The Lime Orchard Woman

The Lime
Orchard Woman

Poems by

Alberto Ríos

THE SHEEP MEADOW PRESS
Riverdale-on-Hudson, New York

All inquiries and permission requests should be
addressed to:
The Sheep Meadow Press, Post Office Box 1345,
Riverdale-on-Hudson, New York 10471.

Distributed by: The Sheep Meadow Press.

Printed on acid-free paper in the United States. This book
meets the guidelines for permanence and durability of the
Committee on Production Guidelines for Book Longevity of
the Council on Library Resources.

Library of Congress Cataloging-in-Publication Data

Ríos, Alberto.
    The lime orchard woman: poems / by Alberto Ríos.
        p.   cm.
        ISBN 0-935296-77-8
        1. Title.
    PS3568.I587L56   1988
    811'.54–dc19   88-18534
                                                          CIP

Second Printing 1994

For Joaquín

For nothing more than to know the simple taste
Of having sons.

Acknowledgments

The following poems first appeared in these journals and
anthologies:
American Poetry Review: "Saints, and Their Care." *Black Warrior
Review:* "Street, Cloud." *Blue Buildings:* "One Woman Turns Her Lips
Away," "Playing." *Crazyhorse:* "The Sword Eusebio Montero
Swallowed, and Kept There." *5 A.M.:* "The Industry of Hard
Kissing." *Ironwood:* "He Will Not Leave a Note," "Mason Jars by the
Window," "What She Had Believed All Her Life." *Journal of Ethnic
Studies:* "Remembering Watching Romy Schneider," "The Vietnam
Wall," "City Dance," "Nikita," "Piece for Flute and Clarinet," "One
Winter I Devise a Plan of My Own," "Stepping Over the Arm," "Like
This It Is We Think to Dance." *Mississippi Review:* "The Lime
Orchard Woman." *North American Review:* "The Corner Uncle."
Occasional Review: "Mr. Disney's Animation." *Ohio Review:* "The Night
Would Grow Like a Telescope Pulled Out," "Juan Rulfo Moved
Away." *Paris Review:* "Horses, Which Do Not Exist." *Prairie Schooner:*
"Edith Piaf Dead," "Sculpting the Whistle," "Shoreline Horses."
Riversedge: "Carnival on South Sixth." *Sonora Review:* "Table
Manners," "Secret Prune," "The Man, Fat and Cigar." *2+2:* "First
Words," "I Drive While Kissing You," "Winter Whiskey." *Western
Humanities Review:* "Concerning an End to His Life." *Willow Springs:*
"Miguelín and His Best Idea." *Up Late:* "Incident at Imuris."

Some of these poems have also appeared in a limited edition, *The
Warrington Poems* (Pyracantha Press).

Grateful acknowledgment is given to Arizona State University for
a faculty grant, during which period some of these poems were
written.

Contents

ONE

TWO

THREE

FOUR

The Lime Orchard Woman

One

The Industry of Hard Kissing

Knocking cows over when they sleep
They get mad.
Ordinary life falls the quickest
Is the easiest to make
Breathe hard,
The quiet of a sad desire
For someone
You cannot have
Again, this small cancer
Of the happy soul.
So we kiss harder, or
Not at all, something
Saved for the other,
For the whistles and the cheeses
Of another life,
Another mouth.
And a thousand new words suddenly
Are what you must say now
Instead of *the other woman*
Since there is no other woman
And there is.

He Will Not Leave a Note

Mariquita awoke one morning
Before the alarm of birds.
She sat up and considered
The face of the long man next to her:
Mouth open, sheet marks and hair
Obvious on his skin.
He was a shaving man, single blade
Fitting into the timeless schemes:
His face was like each of the oceans,
A measurable tide of hair
Coming up from his chest at night.
It receded signaled by a hundred-watt moon,
This hair given over to another gravity
As later she rinsed the sink. This
He called shaving, and was something
He decided early in life like his father to do.
But Mariquita thought to herself this morning
That he was only fooling himself,
Impatient boy, that he had not after all
Watched his father to the end.
The hair soon enough would recede anyway
Starting slowly with his head
At the point where he had grown tallest.
His head spoke this clue
As still in his sleep he turned his back to her
And on the back of his head she saw
The secret place, barely visible,
A clearing under the growth for night things,
For dreams to come just farther than allowed.
He had never told her about it
The same way exactly he had not said
He would be leaving her today.
But she knew. He had not said words,

Given even a hint, no rose on his lapel
The way spies find each other.
Fall was here now, and the wind was loud.
She could hear the outside plainly.
The plants would have to be brought in.
This was October, that feeling, and November.
She would wake to him again tomorrow.
And he would leave her, again, for good.
Every day he was leaving her,
But just a little at a time.
Every day he shaved off something of himself.
One day he would be altogether different.
One day she would wake, and look at
The back of a man who was not there.

Sculpting the Whistle

The machine is in us,
It is what after all makes us pick up,
Make a sound like the sound
We have just heard—
Something of the animal in us,
The mynah—
    What the Japanese call eight songs—
The parrot, and all the zoo,
Some thing of the sculptor—
    Do you know the story of the sculptor
    Who sculpts the whistling
    Sound of the ¡ay Lazaro! birds
Wanting by hands to make it better,
Or simply remembered.
Making the voice of another animal
Creates the other animal
A little. That echo
Everything gives back,
That mirror for the ears
So that in your absence since childhood
When I say your name
Aloud, a small thing happens.

Shoreline Horses

There is a season:
A red curtain makes a red room

Late in the day, the sun
Wanting in more than a dog.

Mariquita watches the fire
Smoke, pokes it to watch

Old rivers,
Old Q's winding up,

Alphabet gone to dream
In the way those French words go,

The longest ones which begin
Familiar, but finish like a doctor's signature

Unpronounced, a line.
Mariquita, watching the fire

Says to herself aloud
You cannot say

All the way through
A word like *underpants*,

You cannot imagine
They might be brought

One night to a face
Then let to fall awkward

Onto the ground before you,
Think your back could be woven

By his hands into bread
Just baked, the feel of that smell.

That you could go like smoke's rise
To the end of all the words.

He had by accident glimpsed,
He said, *her left breast,*

The point of it
On the inside of the green blouse,

That shoreline
Horse of the new world.

Dressing for Dinner

I imagine a small joy,
A woman, standing
In a shower peeing,
The feel of that,
Other people outside
The small width of the door,
In the living room
Beginning dinner.
They wait for her, a night
Out coming to the movies.
She in the shower,
They with drinks:
I imagine it a secret
Smiling of the body,
But I cannot know
For certain. I am a man.
Standing next to her
In the shower
I still cannot know,
Even when she laughs,
Says *yes, yes it is very.*
I can only imagine,
Hold myself close
To my own leg,
Feel the warming go down.
I can only pretend
I am a woman.

Mason Jars by the Window

Yes, but beyond happiness what is there?
The question has not yet been answered.
No great quotations have issued forth
From there, we have no still photographs
Full of men in fine leather hiking boots,
Women with new-cut walking sticks.
    So yes, it is the realm of thin tigers
Prowling, out to earn even more stripes;
It is the smell of seven or eight perfumes
Not currently available in America.
    Maybe this is wrong, of course.
The place may after all be populated,
Or over-populated, with dented trash cans
In the streets and news of genital herpes
In every smart article in every slick magazine
Everywhere in the place.
    But everybody there smiles—
Laughs, even, every time a breath can be caught.
This is all true.
Beyond happiness, it's all the same,
Things come back to where we are now.
Of course maybe this is wrong,
But don't believe it: a happiness exists,
All right, I have seen it for myself,
Touched it, touched the woman
Who with her daughter together keep
Ammonia in Mason jars by the side window.
They will throw it all in his face God
Damn him if he ever comes close again.

The Friday Morning Trial
of Mrs. Solano

A thin man
Like grass blades,
Like mouse hairs,
He knew the color
Of the devil's eyes.
From his beginning
As the loud boy,
Piñatas had made him
Expert at hitting.
Once he had broken
    Open the body of a rose,
Had caught in mid air
A glass piggy bank.
He knew it was falling, had looked
That way one is not allowed
From under the blindfold.
Why Mrs. García put a glass pig
In there, how she could have
Thought it would not break,
No one knew.
He had been angry
To catch it,
Stupid he called her
    To her face.
This was the first thing.

He grew to marry
What he was familiar with:
One more piñata, a wife,
And he had piñatas as well for children.
All of them roses,
All of them he made
Into pieces of roses,
Hard with his ugly hands,
Easy from practice.

Once in a bar to half a friend he said
The best he did was
One summer in a stand of trees
There with a girl
Whose name he could
Not remember, *Josefa, Caras,*
He had breathed into himself
     Her breath
As they had kissed that way,
She said, that way
Of the wettest French women.
He had breathed her in.
And for a moment
He had nothing in his hands.

Gray, he said.
The color of the animal's eyes.
The judge asked him
That first time there was trouble.
He answered *gray,* and that
So was this devil's skin.
That color of the tongues
His children would later let out
     From their mouths.

Gray he would say
After holding a stick in his hands
The last time.

Gray the way he always said,
Talking to her about the devil
All those nights when he had finished
With each of them.
An equal gray, she imagined, to the color
His own eyes turned
The moment she said no to him
With a small gun. No
A hundred times.

Saints, and Their Care

Doña Gabriela made the front
    and biggest room of the house green
As a practical matter and in homage to
The fine framed picture of the painting
La Virgen de Guadalupe, and its coloration
    with which everyone is familiar
As she appeared to Juan Diego the Indian.
The white doilies on the green chairs furthermore
Made a pleasing contrast
With or without their having any inner knowledge
    of the presence of the picture in the room,
The doilies with their lace aspect
    looking like something one supposes
The Virgin must have worn, or desired to wear,
A color she wept from her eyes
Though the picture of the painting did not show it.
Green was her color, but white was her desire:
In her eyes, the way the pupils and irises
    were all business
But then all of the white to the sides
    being what she did in her leisure time
    after supper, after taking care of the dogs
    and having covered the parrot for sleep.
She was a saint, and this is their way,
    - thought Doña Gabriela as she was finished
    with all of the pieces of the room.
To make one look only into the centers of their eyes.

One Woman Turns Her Lips Away

This time, she will not go away so simply.
She, this woman, into whose mouth, whose breathings,
He can see: he closes his eyes: she gives him
Tourniquet kisses,
Saving things, her absolute lips the moment
Holding tightly: everything here is hardened.
And he needs them. Loosening means a dying
Suddenly. Laughter
Too this way is furious, holding something
By its edge, like grasping a carp still living
By its stomach, loving to see it struggle,
Wildishly flipping.
He has held the legs of his women carp-like,
Watched them turn so easily on the fingers,
At his hand and mouth, at his legs: at this minute
Each of his fingers
Knows a different woman, knowing the tinge
Incense gives to rooms, a perfume that travel
Gives to things. But she at his laughter laughs louder.
Quick the exotic
Carp, she turns her animal lips all sticky,
Strong like fingers, stronger than his, not letting
Go: she smells him watching her tight skin, hears him
Curiously flipping.
One man cannot have her, no husband craving
Her, his wife: for each of his fingers she is giving
Gifts of softer skin to the men she's wanted,
All of them handsome.

Street, Cloud

The Phoenix pavement sometimes gets
Away, crawling up to paint
The buildings and many times the sky
With itself, the way an unhealthy dog
Might run its body quickly along the grass.
The woman, having got herself caught
In between the cracks of all this, lies gray
And camouflaged two doors down from the kitchen
That has never touched a new wife's pastry.
She speaks among two men sitting
And I am not surprised to see any of them,
The pavement covering these three
So smoothly, so firmly they fit, natural,
Essential to this place at this moment.
What she says I can only invent for myself,
How important her point must be
Now as she grabs her sack *this* tight,
This bag where inside she has kept from slipping
The private colors of a real day
And one day, today, she thinks of a peach,
The peach color of a frivolous slip,
How once somewhere in the hot southern woods
Like not anyone before ever
He stood her thin body up
Pushed over the tops of her arms the silk straps
And let that thing fall from her.

What She Had Believed All Her Life

Sometime in the night she became afraid
Of noise—loud at first, but then any
So that even the smallest motions of a cat
Unrecognized became noise, and she
Grew smaller, into the folds of the strong sheets,
Like men into the cave-like mines for copper.
As she was shrinking she became as afraid
Of disappearing as she was afraid of noise
The other way, and she wished now
    Only to stay perfectly in between,
    To live there decently
    Suspended better than any carnival trick.
But she could not balance, and whimpered
A loud sound in that moment of falling.
Together they won her this time,
Noise and pain, away and toward.
How this sound could come from inside,
Betraying what she had believed all her life,
That inside at least was a private place, hers,
    As now she heard a noise that would not stop,
    The leopards of the inside forest,
    The spiders that are darkest, all surfacing,
She could not understand, she could not.
And pain, it should not fit there.
She had taken the care to eat too much
For all the days of her tiny breathing
So that nothing more should fit.
    This surprise, this surprise,
    Like a party inside among her organs,
    But before she could fix herself up,
    Before she could plan what to wear.

The Lime Orchard Woman

1

As she grows to twelve, her body begins
Its Spring, its hike along the trail
In the mountains that open
Suddenly to show a whole valley
So surprising one forgets
For the moment to breathe.
Her hips, and so her walk,
Her breasts, and so
The way she begins to see
How other people look at her,
How they are caught mid-breath, and shy.
But the day a train first came here,
They look at her like that:
No one staring at her face, no one
Noting a moustache curling up
Like the arms of the bald
He-man posing in the traveling circus
There on the face of the engineer.
She gets angry, steam in her head
The way the engine had
Barely held in, almost bursting.
Angry in the manner that a person might
Take an egg and hold it too hard.
Her breasts begin to grow,
And she gets angry.
Or, she gets angry,
So her breasts begin to grow.
She cannot remember exactly which.

Her mother had told her
This would come,
But told her so quickly, so much
In a hurry and in a small room,
And with the other things,
She neglected to say that also
They would stop growing,
So they might not.
She would have to wear—
She learns this in a dream—
High heels backward on her feet
To keep a symmetry of balance.
The angrier she gets through the months,
The more worried she feels
At the silliness of how
She has begun to grow two new shoulders,
Of how she will have to wear her shoes,
As bigger, one centimeter at a time,
She sprouts out like buds, at first,
Like fast plants,
Then, like the trees,
And finally unstoppable
In their season: *fruit*.
The future, she reasons, cannot be good.

2

At 28, she has forgotten what is past.
She sits and watches now her thighs
Flowing out like the broad
Varicosed backs of alligators
She has seen in moving pictures,
Pushed out around the metal
Edges of the lawn chair.

Long and flat animals,
Sated and full of wrinkling
Ridges, held as if by small bones
The way camping tents are suspended,
All from having eaten
Too many pigs, too many birds and cows
In the summers of her middle
Years of crying
When she was all mouth and chewing
To feel better, all without boys,
No Pedro of her own
And now the boys cannot
Come close, dare not
Dare the alligators
Which might come after them.

3

But no. This is an exaggeration,
This sadness
At herself. Sadness is like that,
Adding weight to a thing, to legs
The way legs look as one sits
In a chair relaxed,
Or on the edge of a wall.
As if one were a circus performer
With a partner, Ramón, Ramón standing
Feet planted this moment precisely
On the thighs.

But no. This is a further exaggeration.
Sadness again is like that,
It learns you, she thinks,
Makes you heavy in those places exactly
You have dared think to be strong.

On Thursday the 8th of this month
Miguel her husband left her,
But in that odd physics of how distance
Increased every step she took
Away from him.
As she left the house, he got farther.
As she, his María, walked out the door
He left her, and the more she walked
The farther he got, and smaller.
She had learned him as one learns
A pair of good leather shoes.
She loved him so much
She stopped thinking about him.
He was like breathing.
So that when sadness called, she went
To see what it wanted
And did not worry.
Sadness, again, is like that,
Not telling a person the whole story.

4

The orchard was his passion now
More than women,
More than hard words and fast guns
In the hands of other men.
And he tended his trees with fingers
He might have used touching
The hair of his young cousin, lovely
María, his wife, light skinned,
Eyes the color in the moss
And barks of his trees,
Who walked to the river and stayed.

Fingers that might have
Pointed out to her with care
The beaten line a trail made
Leading to his house, their house.
But he was busy growing the limes
So that her hair was like a bramble
Having to be torn away
Hard from her, leaving the blood.

All of this she said to him,
And it was true, or not true.
In a day or a week she would know.
Sadness was in her
Growing like the unstoppable breasts
Again, but it would stop.
As it had learned her,
She had learned it.
She knew only that next
She would have to get the high heels—
The dream had come again.
Put them on backward
To keep a symmetry of balance
For what she wanted to do:
Walk backward, to the moment
Her breasts were those small animals,
Just big enough
To touch him with their mouths
Not angry.

Two

Two

Incident at Imuris

Mr. Aplinio Morales has reported this:
They were not after all
Watermelons, it was not the wild
Fruit patch they at first had thought;
In the manner of what moths do,
These were cocoons, as every child has
Picked up and squeezed,
But from in these came and they saw
Thousands of green-winged half moths,
Half moths and not exactly butterflies,
Not exactly puppies—
A name for them did not exist here.
Half this and some of that,
What was familiar and what might be European.
And when the fruit rotted, or seemed to rot—
Almost all of them on the same day—
From out of each husk the beasts flew
Fat, equipped, at ease
So that they were not so much
Hungry as curious.
The watermelons had been generous homes.
These were not begging animals,
Not raccoons, nor rats,
Not second or third class;
These were the kind that if human
They would have worn dinner jackets
And sniffed, not at anything in particular,
Just as general commentary.
Animals who had time for tea.
Easily distracted and obviously educated
In some inexplicable manner,

The beasts of the watermelons left
The same day, after putting their heads
In windows, bored already
From chasing the horses
And drinking too much from the town well.

First Words

By itself the piano was playing a waltz.
The old couple had been left just then with an orphan
And they told him, *this is a wooden cricket.*
The boy called out at once, far too loudly he knew,
It's not the way things used to be.
People were happy with plain crickets.
He had never seen anything quite so alone.
They asked, *what are you crying for, small boy?*
To them he knew he had to answer.
I should have controlled myself, of course.
The future of myself depends on it.
But the cricket's voice he thought was like the forest,
And each of the notes played from that paper list were people
Who had lost their nations, and consequently their health.
I've had a knack for book-learning, he said.
And that's how I know about things.
They looked at him and saw it was true.
How long have you had your infirmity, and
Were you born so? He nodded his head to say yes.
They were he could tell both embarrassed,
Able only to drop into the single words of children.
The man of the couple came over to apologize
For all the things that had ever been wrong,
And quietly the boy nodded again, yes,
Hugging carefully the man's crooked back.

The Sword Eusebio Montero Swallowed, and Kept There

On a day early in September, 1938, Eusebio Montero the great Venezuelan baritone living out the end of his life in Mexico sprayed his throat, rolled his shirt cuffs, and stepped out to face an oncoming tornado, deciding after seeing his neighbors terrified enough was enough.

1

So wide was the song
This man sang out
Firmly from his fixed mouth
The music made delicate paths,
Ribs in the earth.
Topsoil and debris moved
To the side just like that.

Needing work done the town fathers
Having as was often the case no money
Called on him:
Three songs *forte*
And a small warehouse was finished,
Brought down artfully
In the last second of the last minute
Of a dramatic and building refrain.

Opera like his was a weapon
And so he never made his name
Touring the European circuit
Knowing a voice like this
In the manner of a sword
Must be kept sheathed,

Worn to the side.
Singing for friends he hummed
Only, and this was enough.
Anything worn on a head was held
Or else if for instance it were a hat
The owner could find it
Pinned to a back wall.
So many sometimes and so flat
The hats had an aspect
Butterfly collections present.
Generous of spirit,
If the maestro saw this
He would hold a last note
A full minute longer than usual
That the guest might go to the wall,
Take his hat,
Have a word with a neighbor
And never have to stoop.

2

When the tornado came
It was his destiny:
Standing at the edge of town,
A town which had just seen
The birth of live twins,
He sang angling his voice
Clockwise against it,
All night and into the morning
Until he made, and this is fact,
The wind a baby as well.

Some attributed to these heroic hours
Something more than just a beating
Up of the wind:
This tornado was they said
A large wood-nail
Trying to find its home in metal.
Unable, it danced all around in the night
Making noises and breathing heavy.
Eusebio, they whispered, very low,
With his voice
Had made The Carpenter weary.
Though no one but Eusebio knew Italian,
Italy where the Pope is,
He said, they felt certain,
Nothing is loose here.
Take your wood-screw away.
Take your dirty workbag of clouds.
This was, they worried,
A step too far.

3

No one ever knew
His name: Eusebio Montero
Simply had a ring to it
And was not a name
Otherwise in use at the time,
Though everyone thereafter came to have
Some part of the name as his own,
Eusebia, Terito the suspected dwarf,
The only other set of twins
Sebo and his brother,
Also known as Sebo,
Creating some confusion,

Each however as adults
Calling himself *Sebo's brother.*

He did have a real name,
But so long,
When he spoke it all at once
A person found himself
High like his hat
Flat against the wall
On the other side of the room
Too surprised, too groggy, to remember
Anything the baritone had said.
Eusebio Montero was a nice enough name.
They gave it to him,
A necessary gift,
And he understood.

4

A few days later in that September
His mother called him
Who was dead, and so had a louder voice.
M'ijo, she said, *come home.*
To his friends who had gathered
Eusebio said
What else was there to do?
His only lot was complaint,
As if he were a boy again,
And he began, mama this, mama that:
Eusebio was only sometimes a good son.
For weeks they heard
As his mother pulled him away
By the hands.
Then the late fall rains began,
And it was thunder.

Carnival on South Sixth

The lightning, overhead, the lightning,
Two boys stand before the ride is over
But a voice-whip stings them back
At the slow moment of thunder.
A man with an unbalanced head
And half-hanging moustache
On his face like Florida on the map
Frowns over a black tee-shirt pocket
Stuffed like a small fish with red tickets.
He stops the ride
Lifting the safety bar
With a single forearm snap.
There is, they know, a tattoo somewhere:
They can see it with something
Not their eyes.
The man in the cotton candy booth is smiling,
Nobody stops smiling in the electric,
The Arabian tents, everybody smoking.
Underneath the concession counters
They are all holding hands:
Their fingers, the boys see, are long
Metal umbilical cords all over
The storming summer South Tucson ground.
Wet, standing near the teddy bears
Hung and dead like tough-bearded men
Scratched with steel laugh lines
Inherited like an appendix,
The boys wait for the Ferris wheel to leave its track
The night when everything will be free
The owners celebrating
The fifth anniversary of their getting rich.

They watch from a corner the steel-nippled wonder
Woman in a wet cotton tank top
Giving change for a dollar in dimes only,
Desire's envoy to the city.
Then, in a snail arpeggio
The lights go off the rides
But South Tucson stays,
Two boys standing in the rain.
Everything is closed. From the houses
More people than were here all night
Come to stare at a thing asleep
From a distance, women pointing,
Men in cowboy hats.

The Night Would Grow Like a Telescope
Pulled Out

People would come to my great-grandmother's house.
She was in a room. They would stay in the kitchen.
The words their words rolled like cars by on a train
Here from somewhere else and going somewhere else
Moving on faster almost than we could read them,
Sound them out my brother and me with our small mouths,
Chessie, a cat, see? the Erie, Santa Fe, Ferrocarril,
Ore cars from the Southern Pacific, brown
And all the numbers of all the engines.
    The words they rolled easier, fat and longer
With each beer held in a fist and hit
Against brown lips and thin tongues,
And things slid out of those mouths then with the drinking,
Took shape in sounds larger than we were, those uncles' laughs,
Loud things which could be called back no longer.
    The words they rolled into plates of food
Up with the smoke curling, there around the elbows, the words
And the smoke, a tablecloth, a rope wound like a hypnotist's wheel
All of it catching the heads of our mother in weak headlocks
That fooled us—we had thought we were stronger
With our thousand gatling short words,
Half tears, half whispered. We were not.
    The words they rolled their wheels they rolled
Until the mayonnaise turned light and then dark brown
Until we slept in the corners, my brother and my cousins,
Me with Midnight and Puerquito, our own hands
Held around ourselves, our voices intimate
Only with the animals, who understood something of us,
Who let us hold their heads to our chests,
Who looked at the things we whispered.
    The words, they rolled, they, they would not stop.

I closed my eyes then, and their phrases became birds,
Long birds, fat, snake birds that would not fly.
A single laugh, some thin tongue pulled to its shrill
Kicking roots, this one laugh, an uncle's,
It was the thinnest and strongest string
Pulling their faces up together like puppets
And they hit each other, those wooden heads
Laughing, hit each other rolling, blunt-edged
Side hitting sides like rocks and pieces of hill
Heading along toward some bottom, heading
Somewhere, the place of the broken parts.
Nothing would take me by the hand, only the handle
On the drawer in the corner, my hand holding it, my eyes
Seeing how it became a licorice stick, then thousands of them
Holding me, by the eyes, so I could see nothing,
Hear only the sounds of a second world
In league with the thunder and this night of summer.
The words, they rolled, they would not stop,
They would not take me home.

Singing the Internationale

We heard the stories big-screen like,
Martí did this, Sandino over there,
Jara later without his fingers,
How the *Internationale*'s words were
Meant to be sung.
They were all the never quite in front of us,
The invisible and secret,
Aunts and uncles, José, César,
Victor Jara who was, possibly, my grandfather,
Or his brother, which did not so much matter.
What counted was when he played the mandolin
Once on a train as a musician—
This is what he said he was,
Not a lawyer, which was fact—
And so escaped the Villista's bullet,
But with a rifle held
To his temple as he played.
And the great Doroteo Arango himself,
My wandering great-uncle
On the other side of the family,
Who dropped his coffee once
Staining the rug of my Great-aunt Gabriela,
Her only rug, and so she scolded him,
With force. *Pancho Villa indeed,* she said.
And he had to come back to face the debt.
She made him promise.
Desgraciado, she called him, and pinched
His fat ear in the beak of her two fingers.

Mr. Disney's Animation

My cousin Eddie didn't like his food
Managing daily to hide it
Securely under his unstylishly
    wide collar.
But then one day
His mother in a fit shook him.
The night's meal, and then others—
Whole dinners came down
That hadn't come out in the wash,
    liver, mushrooms, a tongue.
She had figured he was beginning a hunch-back,
And had been planning to seek expert
Medical advice in the city.
    That very Thursday in fact.
Unnecessary now, the hump came down
The way pictures quickly thumbed
In a glossy menu seem to move, alive almost
After the mysterious fashion
    Mr. Disney's animation provided.
Together they stared
At this shambled deli.
She tapped her foot.
    He pretended it was not his.
Stern, breathing perfectly controlled,
Lips firm, she removed her apron.
She stared until he had to turn away.
    She did not say okay, all right,
And swing him up to her bosom
And brush his hair with her hand,
The way he hoped.
He had, instead, gone the step too far,
The way she warned him that one day
He would.
    She said only, *eat.*

The Corner Uncle

He has listened to his records
So much they are scratched,
So much he must believe now
Chopin is performed in the rain,
That the *Nocturnes* all along
Had been missing
Some section of orchestra.

I listen with him sometimes, hum,
Remember with him what he remembers:
How the spear-tip hair of his temples
Used to catch under his moose's brows,
Keeping them from moving almost,
The way screen door latch mechanisms
Might, determining the potential
For movement on his face: only
Smiling was very dangerous.
Because, he explained to me,
When he did, his brows would go
Up, his temple hair would slide and hit
His eyes like a sharp finger,
And this was no good at all,
So he laughed only at extreme wit,
Thereby keeping his ordered face
Scientifically from falling
In parts to a pile on the floor.

But the hair on his head
Has been through the years
Like a glass of beer drunk down,
Receding as if carefully sipped
Until the taker is filled,
And the head left empty
But for the spots and bits at the bottom.

In the parking lot of the Public Library
The brownbaggers pee themselves out
In front of us all
Until they're hollow and can't stand.
I watch, and when I get home
I watch myself, the falling line of me,
Myself a little less, I feel it.

Uncle Maclovio's Secret, Never to Tell

With immediacy this boy closed his eyes
Every time his mother turned out the lights:
It was the law
And he was a soldier.
Maybe not a law: he never saw it written, after all.
But a secret, then.
Even better. He closed his eyes
And held them tight until he fell asleep
Or the sun came up, over the mountain outside
Through the curtains, past the wood rail
Nailed to the foot of his bed,
Up his own foot, up the covers
To his eyes, making everything red.
    Because if he didn't
    He knew what would happen.
He had dreamed of keeping his eyes open once,
And had seen the face of night as the end
A vacuum cleaner hose presents:
Big round mouth, all black hole and sharp edges,
Something behind it inhaling
He weighing nothing at all
Getting sucked right in:
Pulled inside out faster than
The sleeves of a shirt:
It might almost have been funny
But his uncle Maclovio told him
Every night with his own small mouth
Through the very thin moustaches
Parted off center where the scarring was,
And so this was the way of things,
More than true now because he was dead,

Two winters already, came the news from the south.
Dead from forgetting just once,
Pulled, the whispered and tongue-clucking
Half-reports had said,
Inside out like a sock in his bed.

Miguelín and His Best Idea

Miguelín washed his own mouth out with soap
Every afternoon for a week.
He knew he would be in trouble for what he had done:
He had only wanted to make sounds in the air
But he had broken his grandfather's fork,
Had grabbed and swung its handle too much
Like a sword.
    This was like the snake bites—
    Take this venom, the doctor said
    Once after he had trusted a red snake too much;
    Take it and gradually you will become immune.
He would be tough like that.
His mother with her old trumpet told him loud
If he ever did this again—
He had, after all, done this many times,
Imagined himself a hero of the dishwashers—
She would wash his mouth out
With soap—so he would get ready,
Make himself into a soap callous, a tough stomach.
A man.
    But no one found out, and his mother never did
    Wash his mouth out with soap for anything—
    She just said she would, and he had believed her,
Understanding only many years later
    He learned to hold his nose and eat white soap
    For nothing more than to know the simple taste
    Of having sons.

One Winter I Devise a Plan of My Own

The leaves come here to meet, they fall and bump
The fences of a second life, they drop

Like teeth have gone from me; I've tried to stop
Their plan, but they have mounded up like stumps

Along a ploughing field not readied yet.
A neighbor comes to help, but I refuse

His hands, I've waved him back; he goes, confused
At first, but then he stops to watch, forgets

Intentions that he might at first have had.
He smiles as I get right down on my knees,

Pretend I'm searching for a coin or key,
Then jump the biggest mound, and bruise it, bad.

Now they have got to climb back on my trees.
Today I've tricked the captain of the leaves.

Three

Remembering Watching Romy Schneider

Her nose, doorstop, small butte
On the floor of a canyon rising.
An explorer standing there must choose
As men through the centuries in stories
Have chosen: cave to the left, cave
To the right, which to the woman?
In the other sits the diseased lion
Drooling, but trying to be quiet
A big fine fat paw to his mouth
Like a napkin
Muffling the ha ha ha of his thoughts.
But the woman there, the woman
Is everything:

That she stepped no shoe a nyloned foot
Hard to the sand,
Kissed me like no one
On the eyes, her chest to my shoulders
Where the real kiss was,
And warm—I was young, cereal, and soldiers,
Consomme soup, class roll, a fast car,
Faster hands, two Slavic secrets—
That boys like me dreamed of
Girls like her, luck and
Time, a blanket, protection, a next time, everything—
We called it just Skin, but thought really
Nipples—chocolate cake mix
Full of batter bits and flecks, that skin,
So much thinking That Skin
Finally one eye per nipple
Just was not enough,
One eye and one hand, one arm and one ear,

Never were just enough to cover
In that way we wanted to cover
With our whole being
The mighty, secret, small nipple
Of a girl.

Is why we all have married,
Eat chicken, date
And have manners, don't get ahead
In movie lines, those lines
Wherein one must choose: which movie.
Which to the lion, which to the woman
Always hoping for the woman
Who on the screen has nostrils so big
An explorer watching might enter,
Carve initials, an arrow and a date,
Then go.

I Drive While Kissing You

Riding car top down
On an Arizona road
Sunsets are a dime a dozen.
Hard times die here
Where the boys are men
And the women ride horses
Where they want.
Riding car top down
A car goes faster.
Everybody weighs less
And the stars
Pack a spark like a pin.
Everybody who used to be
Old now isn't,
And cows by the road
Make us laugh.
The road lights up
And the people let us through.
The road goes up
And won't come down.
I've taken a ride
Through the night
And the night is you.
Riding car top down
All steel and song,
I am the man
And the boy you knew.

Piece for Flute and Clarinet

This music somewhere:
Drifts in from the street
Fourth wall of the room,
    thin, maybe Brazilian at first
Samba on the sand beneath a light,
    a quiet and evening sun
Settling at dusk all at once into shadow,
Into the tight tango strain
    of the nervous night, high strung
        suddenly gathered at the neck:
A thousand moons in the single sky,
A flute, a clarinet,
    a girl who will cry.

In the house, music, and the light
White curtains.
An open window.
No morning here,
As in a Jobim song,
Only afternoons, late
    and that which follows,
And always sand, always clean
    bare and hot and moveable
As if that part of the eye
Central and dark
For seeing into darkness
Is ignored finally, swallows
    itself up
And the world
    it sways
        it moves as if again
It is young
    and wants to be.

I am sitting on a couch
Dreaming of the outside.
Ten things, ten songs,
    ten parts of a long woman
And the woman always walks
    complex, tight
Ten parts in a leg
    the back of a head
And the hair that she holds with her hand.

Secret Prune

1

In that small way of things and of wonder
The pit of a sweet prune after sucking fell open
In my mouth, and its center I found
Made itself up of two nuts, which I chewed.
I recognized the taste in that second:
The taste of snow cones, of Mexico
In the summer on a walk through Magdalena.
Seeing Father Kino's bones.
It was the toy taste of plum dried,
Which didn't exist anywhere
Except in that this flavor was called
In Mexico, *ciruela*. The pretend taste
Carnivals had been hiding as a gift
For patience, thirty-one years.
There in prunes, in their middle.
The one place no one would look.

2

Come with me to the country.
I know another secret:
Rain hitting the dry bean pods
On the mesquite, a *maracas*
Music, every tree for miles
When rain has been slow in the desert,
Sounding out like castanets hit
All at the same time
By the twelve women dancers, in a row,
Then all of the heels of the men.
A loudness like locusts,
All of them happy.
Beatniks applauding, a farm woman
Calling to each of her goats.
This was my gift at twenty-nine.
I remember them all.

Like This It Is We Think to Dance

Hips to hips Elvis in our hearts the hearts
  Beating in our legs, Portuguese in our mouths
    We dance the slow dance of trees-near-fire frenzy
      The crawl of silk worm, the hand beginning down a blouse
      The slow that wants to be fast
      That could be lovemaking

Hips to hips swaying we touch ourselves
  To ourselves in a toast of slow champagnes
    Our eyes swaying, with a view pendulums must have
      Swaying even with spring trees and light wind
      Swaying, forth and back, back then push
      Point to point and we do not break

Hips to hips hit of the champagne glass we put ourselves
  To ourselves forward, in that going way of terrier snout
    There after a mouse in the field, but slow
      An elephant, doing the last circus work of the night
      Head-strong still: *Saturnino el magnífico*
      Putting away, pushing against the backdrops and boxcars

Hips into the night away swaying still with the thinking
  Of the grocery store horse ride of our being five
    Of the nickel and the slot and the waiting and the bucking
      Jukebox of our bodies, Like this it is we think to dance
      Jump in our legs the legs our hard tongues are, running
      Into each other with the fingers of our ten hands on us

Practicing the Cornet

Today rain, the raining,
The thinking of your wrists
No bracelets but for skin
Folds, marks, decorative
Braiding lines, folds
Like no other, like folds
Not at all.
Today the rain
Like no other
Thinking of no one
Else, your wrists
And your hands and the nose
Those hands touch,
The lips. The rain
I hear it.
I could feel it if
I walked out there.

The Fact of Their Two Bodies

I think about my youngest cousin loving a boy
With kisses, with her eyes and her small bones,
So many flutes, so much the sounds of a music
Inside, so many little noises when he hugs her.
I cannot imagine it well, or do not want it:
This moving picture of two nude children
Running to the forests of the cool north
Happy at last: concert, clapping, laughing.
Them rolling on the ground all over
Into themselves, farther than their eyes
Can see, hands into themselves
Pulling out the rabbits of fine surprise.

Him, pulling off her blouse fast
As a tablecloth, only a little movement
Of her delicate dishes, her two china teacups,
This small, a nickle's worth of magic.

Her thin legs: wide, open arms to hold him,
Welcome and hello him *my own true love.*
Happier and wilder, stronger, stranger
Happier and unhappier
Than any of us.

And what your skin must smell of.

Edith Piaf Dead

I have a young cousin who is fire.
Myself married, Edith,
I would have given him to you.

I have seen the picture,
The one always shown—she is
A glint in the pupil of an eye,
An eye, like this: we in the cheap seats
White, yellowish almost, garish
Lined against the blues and browns,
The evening wear of the monied.
Pupil, black center, the stage
Not yet lit.
    Then she. A chip.
A nicking in the wood of a counter
Almost not worth the notice
So that one must see with full attention:
Stomach tightening, eyes getting hot
That way of a hard stare:
She is an imperfection
As a nick or a chip is a moment of pain:

Wood splinter caught under a nail,
A banged elbow, or a blouse caught
    By the hand of a man.

And then, you know. The pictures
Or the stories, you know:

That voice coming out like scarves
From a magician's sleeve
Finishing with the underwear, and laughs.
But then the hairs under that, and
The bone, the pubis, the mouth there
Singing too the same exact songs.
Loud.

I have dreams about you Edith Piaf.
How much I don't want to cry in my own life.
A voice comes out like scarves.

Nikita

Under a heavy wire milk case,
A piece of concrete foundation
On top, in summer, in her backyard,
Mrs. Russo keeps the cat Nikita safe
From birds, from dogs, from eating
Johnson grass, which he throws up.
Nikita waits for ants to wander in
And for the sun to leave.
Instead, she comes to keep him
Company, saying You look fat
And that her son died,
Remember I told you?
Walking thin in his uniform
On a road.

The Vietnam Wall

I
Have seen it
And I like it: The magic,
The way like cutting onions
It brings water out of nowhere.
Invisible from one side, a scar
Into the skin of the ground
From the other, a black winding
Appendix line.
    A dig.
    An archaeologist can explain.
The walk is slow at first
Easy, a little black marble wall
Of a dollhouse,
A smoothness, a shine
The boys in the street want to give.
One name. And then more
Names, long lines, lines of names until
They are the shape of the U.N. building
Taller than I am: I have walked
Into a grave.
And everything I expect has been taken away, like that, quick:
    The names are not alphabetized.
    They are in the order of dying,
    An alphabet of—somewhere—screaming.
I start to walk out. I almost leave
But stop to look up names of friends,
My own name. There is somebody
Severiano Ríos.
Little kids do not make the same noise
Here, junior high school boys don't run
Or hold each other in headlocks.

No rules, something just persists
Like pinching on St. Patrick's Day
Every year for no green.
     No one knows why.
Flowers are forced
Into the cracks
Between sections.
Men have cried
At this wall.
I have
Seen them.

A Photograph from the Revolution: Guaymas to Nogales

—A photograph from the Mexican Revolution exists in which as far as one can see into the distance men have been hung from every telephone pole.

One woman weeps, and shouts,
gets sick on the sand, slumps against
a gray and greasy maguey plant.
Past praying, picked by its tiny
teeth, she is too tired to bother
as the blood bakes. Her back is numb.

Her husband is hanging; ahead, another
hundred husbands hang with him.
Women are wandering, new widows, heavy
with hunger, with heat. Here the Cause
flies its flags. A fever moves
among these mothers, making noise.

Four

Nogales, 1958

The black birds at Bank's Bridge fly
Out from underneath at quitting time,
5:00 in a small town, for everyone.
And the town makes its way home.

The paperboys come out, wiry and clear.
Everybody in a car buys a *Herald*.
On the way home you cannot help but see
Someone you know, who will wave.

My brother is three years old.
The green Zenith Moderne is on low:
Someone is singing something, slowly.
A smell of wet woodsmoke borrows the air.

My father will come
Driving the light green 47 Chevrolet,
Dragging its round-back dowager's hump.
My mother is cutting limes for the rice

And I am watching. Today I have watched
The washing machine go around,
And smelled it. That is best,
Lifting its lid just a little.

I have watched the girls coming
Home from school with books held
Against their small chests.
They talk about boys that way

Everyday, holding something in their arms.
And that is all.
Evening comes, and nothing else happens
More than dinner, the news,

One page in a coloring book about trees.

Winter Whiskey

What pass for leaves at a look
Fly by, are black birds,
A group large in the distance
Behind the pecan trees, bare stem
Cracks on the cook's favorite bowl
Of a sky. It is winter,
The leaves go south
And the afternoon opens up.
What the trees have begun
Night takes on, and forces,
    Itself reaching through
    The openings, ripping
Down and through and off
The light blue, dim stretch
Of old slap-on,
Sucker paint to sell a house fast,
Night, with a grin.
And it is night, or afternoon
    Or this year, and love
And birds and leaves and government
All matter, but now I, drunk,
Can't say them like you anymore.
Pecan trees, I'm looking:
All in a row, thousands, so that if
I move my head left very fast to
Right, it's a cartoon,
It's only one tree
Moving its arms a lot. You've seen
Those signers for the deaf onstage,
Like that.
Or else just only the goddam
    Greatest wind-up pitch in the world.

Horses, Which Do Not Exist

The strong horseshoe shape of a horse's mouth
Of his teeth, set that way of a suitcase handle

And the way a bit, in just that way, pulls him:
Come here to where it is I say. Like that

A horse's mouth, and so his manner, broken
Those horses no longer running along the far

Distance visible from a Tucson highway thirsty
Stopping for water, making one of those paintings

Living rooms wear as pendants. Those paintings
Too unreal, laughed at and finger-poked

And so these horses too must be unreal,
A bad painting of nine,

A pond of browning water. Birds, two kinds.
Grass too green—spring has come this year,

And water—mountains too blue, too many shades,
In the distance. And so they are, this all is,

As children say, like a dream,
Laughing hard at how good it seemed at the moment.

Concerning an End to His Life

One can't tell anything by his books.
He did, after all, collect
Everything other people left
So when the chief detective comes,
Says *aha* I will tell something
About the ending of this small man
By the kinds of books he kept
The detective will be wrong, deciding
This man was insane or red socialist,
Or simply unhappy: he finds
In a library of otherwise paperback books
Two accidental cloth volumes
By suicides of note.
The detective will have to say
This, of course, is why he died.
Thinkers are too easily done in.
But the books, all of them
Topped equally by a little dust
Had nothing to do with his ending.
Like each of us he had a woman's heart
Stuck plain in his thick man's body
But couldn't begin to explain to anyone
Because he was afraid more than anything
That another man like himself
Would be called over and have to pretend
Convincingly that he didn't understand.

The Man, Fat and Cigar

Today he is dressed.
Having stepped into a painting
And because it is a Monet,
Everything moves around him.
No one has lit his cigar
But he holds it out of habit.
He had been a healer, this man,
Who touched people hard on the head
With the C-clamp of his fingers.
Not anymore.

With his eyes open
He is remembering, as he remembers
Often, the lady
Who near the end hid her eyes
Behind wrinkles when she laughed
Because she was ashamed
To laugh at anything
After the things in her life
She had seen.
And he had told her,
Be ashamed.

The cat as a noise comes in
And finally he turns
The body too heavy for turning
To see, what? That lady.
She moves around the room
Slowly until he sleeps,
Thinking how many times
He had kissed this woman.
This is what she looked like,
How her eyes disappeared.

The next morning he wakes.
He is in Morocco again.
The common home of things old
And without Christian names,
Weeds around buildings
At night covered by stars
Not part of any constellation.
This is where he lives now,
He thinks. He thinks this
Again, and he cries.

Table Manners

She blows in my ear
Because it looks she says
Like the wrinkled open end
Of a big and sad balloon.
I am thinking of the diviner
Who came in a parole suit
Too gray, too carelessly big,
How he broke a willow
In one motion at the joint
Where it looked most like
The center of a woman.
I was strong-skinned and young.
I followed him secretly
A quiet convert
After he had found the spring
In front of them all.
But he had learned well
The ancient Turkish trick
Of using screeting peahens
Instead of black watchdogs
And under the splintering window
He caught me looking.
Not gently, but like a strong wind
Sometimes seems to have hands,
He took me inside
And there was a woman.
Like numeral eights leaning
Almost into infinities,
The dirty soles of her thin feet
Faced me, familiar and unfamiliar.
And I thought feet look different
From the bottom, but too quickly.

I stared at more, up first, more,
Her almost candy nipples
Raised through a thin blouse
Stained it seemed underneath,
Then other nipples
From how his hands had made on her
Their physical fictions,
His putting the world right
By rearranging it, damming
And clearing, saddling,
Making it understandable to him
Like a game of baseball or baskets.
Back in this room I am cold
Like the feeling of being caught.
At anything.
I lie here and remember him,
Seeing at this moment a game
Of baseball, how it is
A boy's kind of table manners.
I touched each base carefully.
I choked my bat
And grew successfully swift,
Polite and vicious,
And sometimes baseball itself
Makes no sense at all.
Everything that was childhood.
I cease to be polite then.
She blows in my ear
Because I pay no attention.

Stepping Over the Arm

From the flat lung of a gin night,
From the place where night breathes, eyes
Look out: a thin, pressed mouth, an ear,
A small finger's edge can be seen
Or not; they can fool us, deny
What they are by some wild disguise,
It's not a man there just lying,
Not a someone like you, not me . . .
    From the gin lungs
Of that dark animal who hides—
Or who meant to hide, who had tried
But could not crawl to the alley—
He unholsters the *you fugging*
Half-words, shoots us, shoots everything
    Up from night, his lungs, gin.

On a Day, South Park

The headlines in summer
Come here already familiar,
Where they had been lived,
Passed around now
Like Christmas fruitcakes
Or Japanese tourist fans,
Coaxing the low flame
Charcoal day-heat
That makes slow motion
South Park a fat neck
Sweating, a whole fat man
Moving, uncooled,
So that time is always here
The three iron-heavy seconds
Before an accident,
And an accident here
Is when all things
And always people to watch
Spill like animal insides
Into the pools of the street,
Which is wider here,
Creeping up past sidewalks,
Past yards, this street becoming
One wall of every house.

Past the Holsum Bakery
Making day-old breads
For this place in particular,
A man whose long zipper
Is open to the street and cars
Pees into the brick well
Of a dead, city mesquite.

He is a gray man,
Too old to be black or white.
He lifts himself in his hands
As I pass, pointing at me
The conversation of men,
Wishing I were the dead
Tree he is peeing on,
The steep of my body
In the warm, fallen water
Making a human tea
No one even here will drink.
I am pleased, he thinks,
Aloud with his face,
To make you ugly.

City Dance

Nothing is yet lit up.
This is the consequence
Of falling asleep too early.
No sun, no visible lights.
Cinzano shades are useless
This moment as pigs,
And lights like young daughters
Seem emotionally saved.
There was something about
Peeing last night, every time
Too hard, heavy, too suddenly.
Nothing this morning is left,
This stomach too empty.
No one wakes this early,
No waltzing, no Wagner crescendo,
No screaming like drunks
Or if they do whoever they are
It is nothing social.
No casually finding them,
Not like at night, anywhere,
Going to a bar with a dance
Sawdust floor, sawdust air.
How unnatural specifically
Desiring a woman is made to seem
In the morning, this morning.
Hot, danced out, full
And wanting me.
It is not right to want nothing.
Not right to be awake.

Playing

White, round pigeon dropping
Moon you are perfect.
I carved you a hundred times,
Circles on the sidewalks;
I was playing, the way
On those long Sunday picnics
We carved our long names
Into the silt of Sonoita Creek.
The deeper we scratched them
The faster they caved in
So we caught minnows instead
In waxed milk carton traps;
And we were playing
When we took them home
My brother and I
Capping the mayonnaise jars
Tight, my father said, tight
So the water won't spill
All over the seats of the car.
I have come back today, here
To look for my name.

Instead, this afternoon
Shaded by the wide cottonwoods—
And smell, too, of the trees
And the fluff-seeds dropping
Everywhere my eyes can see—
I find the moon again
Or the bare hint of it
Up there, new moon, almost
Invisible through the leaves
And I think of the sidewalks
Like the creek here near Sonoita,
Like the smell of the creek
And the sand and the air,
The trees themselves, the smell
Of their bark, all of it
Like the man, the smell of the man
I carved my name in,
Too deeply.

Pictures Looked At Once More

August lightning opens the afternoon sky
As one might open an egg.
Opens, or breaks, the same way
Those album photographs get ripped
Then Scotch-taped back together.
The pictures we look at today
They are like that, angry and then soothed,
Good to look at again and nod,
Worth having kept track of.
　　Thunder too is there, a man's voice,
His roll of words, twisting
Fingers in a fist, the moment
Tearing apart more than the photographs.
　　Rain too in the open hand of the sky,
　　The work of rain and sparrows and wind.
These are better photographs
Of what is not there in them:
All the times we cried at having wanted
Something, a father maybe,
To come home, wanted him there
Enough to rip apart.

Juan Rulfo Moved Away

Tonight I am told
Juan Rulfo has died—
If such a thing is possible—
Tuesday last.
We've returned from a party
Watching Halley's comet,
And so should have known.
A heart attack. The way
The comet appeared
In the act itself of exploding,
Trying so hard to get somewhere
That something gets left:
In the cartoons
The way a creature runs so fast
It leaves its eyebrows behind.
A heart attack of the stars.
We have given medicine
    To our new son,
Almost eight weeks old this afternoon.
This boy trying to sleep now
Lying somewhere in between us
All, the sky, Juan Rulfo, my arms.
Juan Rulfo leaving so quickly
He did not pack bags.
I could not have guessed
He would be giving this boy room,
That he would leave as a lesson
The simple end of his book
Where a certain Mr. Paramo collapses
Into a pile of stones
Because he was a bad man.

Listening for Tonight

Today I have stayed with
The noises of the house,
Not music, not the radio as always.
Music like this, this kind of radio:
The kettle beginning, its tongue over teeth
Sound, the furniture truck too slowly
Going by as a June beetle might
The way they almost do not fly when they fly.
Then the creaks from the knees of the house
And the cats, who pay attention, every time.
Small dust blown against the window outside,
That noise I imagine I hear of crashing
In a surf of cellular things.
Shoes have left indentations in the carpet.
This secret catalogue of events:
People who will make noise later in the day,
Preparations of dinner tonight,
The kitchen cupboard opened,
The rocking chair making its name,
Noise of the breath of the woman
Who will sit there in it,
Who will rest at the end of one day's working.
Then the pencil, which will scratch
To destruction the minute structures
A page like this keeps invisible.
Noise that will be;
The rhythm hum of the circular fan;
The man who will drum
His fingertips, drips in the water of his shaving.
The noise this evening is making, and tomorrow,
The pointillist dream of it we can conjure:
This, I have heard the future
By listening.

Poetry from The Sheep Meadow Press

Desire for White
Allen Afterman (1991)

Early Poems
Yehuda Amichai (1983)

Travels
Yehuda Amichai (1986)

**Poems of Jerusalem and
Love Poems**
Yehuda Amichai (1992)

Father Fisheye
Peter Balakian (1979)

Sad Days of Light
Peter Balakian (1983)

Reply from Wilderness Island
Peter Balakian (1988)

5 A.M. in Beijing
Willis Barnstone (1987)

Wheat Among Bones
Mary Baron (1979)

The Secrets of the Tribe
Chana Bloch (1980)

The Past Keeps Changing
Chana Bloch (1992)

Memories of Love
Bohdan Boychuk (1989)

Brothers, I Loved You All
Hayden Carruth (1978)

Selected Poems
Diana Der-Hovanessian (1994)

Orchard Lamps
Ivan Drach (1978)

A Full Heart
Edward Field (1977)

Stars in My Eyes
Edward Field (1978)

New and Selected Poems
Edward Field (1987)

Embodiment
Arthur Gregor (1982)

Secret Citizen
Arthur Gregor (1989)

**The River Serpent and
Other Poems**
Arthur Gregor (1994)

Nightwords
Samuel Hazo (1987)

Leaving the Door Open
David Ignatow (1984)

The Flaw
Yaedi Ignatow (1983)

The Ice Lizard
Judith Johnson (1992)

The Roman Quarry
David Jones (1981)

Claims
Shirley Kaufman (1984)

Summers of Vietnam
Mary Kinzie (1990)

The Wellfleet Whale
Stanley Kunitz (1983)

The Moonlit Upper Deckerina
Naomi Lazard (1977)

Poems of B.R. Whiting
B. R. Whiting (1992)

Flogging the Czar
Robert Winner (1983)

Breakers
Ellen Wittlinger (1979)

Landlady and Tenant
Helen Wolfert (1979)

Sometimes
John Yau (1979)

Flowers of Ice
Imants Ziedonis (1987)

Other Titles from Sheep Meadow

Kabbalah and Consciousness
Allen Afterman (1992)

Collected Prose
Paul Celan (1986)

The Quilt and Other Stories
Ismat Chughtai

Dean Cuisine
Jack Greenberg and
James Vorenberg (1990)

The Notebooks of
David Ignatow
David Ignatow (1984)

A Celebration for
Stanley Kunitz
Edited by Stanley Moss (1986)

Interviews and Encounters
with Stanley Kunitz
Edited by Stanley Moss (1993)

The Stove and Other Stories
Jakov Lind (1983)

Two Plays
Howard Moss (1980)

Arshile Gorky
Harold Rosenberg (1985)

Literature and the Visual Arts
Edited by Mark Rudman (1989)

The Stories and Recollections
of Umberto Saba
Umberto Saba (1993)

No Success Like Failure
Ivan Solotaroff (1994)

Cape Discovery: The Fine Arts
Work Center Anthology
Bruce Smith & Catherine
Gammon, editors (1994)

The Tales of Arturo Vivante
Arturo Vivante (1990)

Will the Morning Be Any
Kinder than the Night?
Irving Wexler (1991)

The Summers of James and
Annie Wright
James and Annie Wright (1981)